COLLINS

GEOFF SAMPLE

garden bird songs
and calls

HarperCollins*Publishers*

ACKNOWLEDGEMENTS

I owe a debt of thanks to the many other sound recordists and ornithologists, who've helped me along the way with my work or whose work I've learnt from, particularly Roger Boughton, a constant source of encouragement and advice. Wildlife sound is such a vast subject, full of variations, forever providing exceptions that either confound or prove the rule – depending on how you look at it; so whatever knowledge I've gleaned has come partly through observation in the field and very much through comparing notes with other enthusiasts. Nevertheless any errors in this work are down to me. I'd also like to offer a special word of thanks to Kyle Turner, Terry Barnatt, Phil Rudkin, David Burton and Roger of course, for allowing me to use their excellent recordings and sending them so promptly when contacted.

I doubt that one can find in any human music, however inspired, melodies and rhythms that have the sovereign freedom of bird song.

Olivier Messiaen – musician and composer

HarperCollins*Publishers*
77–85 Fulham Palace Road
London W6 8JB

The HarperCollins website address is: www.**fire**and**water**.com

Collins is a registered trademark of HarperCollins*Publishers* Ltd.

05 04 03 02

10 9 8 7 6 5 4 3

ISBN 0 00 220214 X

© Geoff Sample 2000

CD produced by DOCdata (UK) Ltd.
Printed and bound in Belgium

INTRODUCTION

If you're fairly new to birdwatching, and think that's the sum of it – watching birds – then you're missing half the pleasure. For birds are among the most accomplished musicians in the world. And that's not just my opinion; many writers and composers through the history of literature and art, from Lucretius in the first century BC to Olivier Messiaen in the 20th century AD, have expressed such sentiments.

Admittedly it's not always obvious or easy to appreciate the full implications of an avian singer's performance, since the hearing of birds has a much finer timing resolution than our own. This means that birds can perceive more detailed pattern in sounds that we might describe merely as twittering, rattles or trills. Researchers frequently use the technique of slowing down recordings, sometimes to a tenth of the original speed, in order to decipher some of this detail; and so often this reveals a much more sophisticated structure than is apparent to our hearing.

But the practical advantage to birdwatchers is that, by listening in to the sonic dimension, you can start to identify different species without squinting through bins or scope – in fact, without even seeing the bird. You become more tuned into the bird life around you without necessarily needing to work hard to get a clear view. Standing on a London suburban station waiting for a train with a friend a few days ago, I was aware of a robin in the ivy behind us from the 'tic' sounds; but when three birds dropped out of the sky with those characteristic sibilant calls, I knew straightaway they were redwings over from Scandinavia for the winter and brought into the city by the cold spell. Your nascent skill may then lead you to start asking questions about a bird's behaviour and hopefully you'll soon be able to understand so much more of the bird world. But it may take a bit of work to get started; and without doubt a 'musical ear' helps.

Don't despair if it all seems so confusing sometimes. It may sound like obvious advice but here goes: build your knowledge step by step. Get familiar with the commonest sounds in your garden and that's a good basis to work from. Many species produce quite a variety of sounds, so there's always something new to add to your knowledge; identifying birds by sound is something that comes with practice – it takes time. Nevertheless the rewards are worth it; it may take a number of years, but imagine how satisfying it is to recognise nearly every sound you hear.

The most difficult point is the start: the whole mix of different sounds is a symphony of the unknown. As you learn the songs and calls one by one, by a process of elimination, it gets easier since there are less unknown sounds and, to a certain extent, less possibilities of what they might be.

Gardens and parks are great places for getting to know birds because garden and park birds tend to be used to people and hence more trusting. Particularly if you're busy doing some gardening; birds seem to realise the human is preoccupied and go about their own business without too much concern. And of course the beauty of getting to know a little bit about the sounds of garden birds is that you can be aware of the birds around you while getting on with your work – and maybe just pausing for a breather to check some sound that captures your interest.

We're lucky in that the list of common garden birds for our area includes some of the finest singers; I'm thinking particularly of blackbird and robin, and possibly song thrush depending on your area and your musical tastes. But it has to be said that garden birds are not necessarily the most straightforward when it comes to learning bird voices. Many are woodland or edge species and sound is particularly good for communication in such habitats, where vision may well be obscured. So many species are very vocal and some, such as the tit family, have developed wide vocabularies of calls.

Recording and production of the CD

Many of the recordings have been edited slightly – usually where intervals between songs or calls have been shortened to make more economical use of the time available on the CD, or to include more variation in a sequence, or occasionally to take out unwanted intrusive noises. There's a mixture of mono and stereo recordings; hopefully that makes for a satisfyingly varied listening programme rather than an erratic mixture.

Unless otherwise stated the recordings were made in Northumberland by myself. And many were made in my gardens. I used to record in the garden when I lived in London, but none of those recordings have found their way onto this CD; the backgrounds tended to be too noisy and the species coverage was quite restricted (though I did see most of the species covered here either in our garden or in nearby parks).

I've done a fair bit of recording in two different gardens in Northumberland over the last five years. The first was in Felton – a village of about 600 people, surrounded by farmland, a mile to the east of the A1 and centred on a single main street (the old A1). We had a tiny patch of garden surrounded by houses, but what a great place to enjoy birdsong – starling, blackbird, greenfinch and goldfinch, siskin, collared dove, swallow and house martin, swifts zipping down the main street. The birds were used to human passers-by and so were really quite approachable. But with the A1 in the distance, the cars on the street, the school playground out the back, strimmers, lawn-mowers and all the paraphernalia of modern life, it was a frustrating place for a sound recordist.

Over the last few years we've been living in a fairly remote Victorian bungalow with a glorious overgrown garden, on an old estate, surrounded by parkland, woods and farmland. There's a marsh and a river close by; and the range of birds has been much more varied here with warblers, woodland birds and quite a few unusual species visiting the garden (redstart being one of my favourites). But these are generally all warier, wilder individuals; no house sparrows, collared doves and only occasional starlings. This is further inland, in a valley under the Cheviot hills, further away from any major roads – a place where it's possible to have a background completely silent from mechanical noise. A glorious sound stage.

Nevertheless we're at the centre of five farms being worked as a unit, so even here there's a fairly continuous stream of combustion engines during the day. But what I hadn't appreciated when we looked at the house was the scattered rookery in the surrounding woodland; the local flock of jackdaws and rooks is never less than several hundred strong, with some larger gatherings, and rarely quiet. So most of the recordings from our garden here, and surroundings, have a background thick with corvid calls – as well as the sheep and cattle. A subtle appreciation of irony comes in handy for the wildlife sound recordist.

Geoff Sample Northumberland, December 1999

Learning bird sounds

So where to begin? I'd suggest a two-pronged attack. Firstly, concentrate on a small group of species that are common in your garden and try to learn their sounds: a good start would be wren, dunnock and robin – songs and calls, since these are probably the commonest sounds through the country and through the year. Do a few moments homework with this guide, then try to recognise the sounds outside in the real world. If you have trouble with the songs of these species, then maybe do some practice on simpler songs with a more regular pattern, such as great tit or possibly song thrush; but remember these species only sing regularly from late winter to late spring or early summer.

But the second exercise is to focus on any distinctive sounds that you regularly hear in your garden or wherever you spend time; try to identify these to the species. With this approach observation probably comes first (with a bit of luck you'll actually see and identify the bird making the sound) and then you can check with the guide for confirmation.

Apart from the really distinctive ones (such as jay screeches or mistle thrush rattles), I think calls can be harder to identify than songs. There are whole areas where there are groups of species that produce similar sounds; 'teuy' of coal tit, siskin, redpoll and 'tooey' of greenfinch and linnet. Don't worry, some of these take time to be able to distinguish.

A few hints

A useful technique for remembering sounds is to form it into a word and spell it in your mind: you may find it easier to remember. Or with more complex sounds, such as song, if it suggests or reminds you of something, remember the association (maybe sad-sounding, zany, or an electronic bleep).

Often the most distinctive characteristic for a species is the rhythm of its calls (e.g. long-tailed tits typically 3–4 'tsee's in a row); or some other aspect of the delivery such as a call usually repeated or rarely repeated.

There are often similarities to the voices (and often style of songs) of species within the same family or even closely related families. Also the average pitch or depth of the voice broadly correlates with size: small birds have high-pitched, thin voices and are physically unable to produce the deeper and lower-pitched sounds that are usual for larger birds.

Describing sounds

At the risk of stating the obvious – birds have rather different voices to us humans. This means that it's rarely easy to transcribe bird sounds and attempts to write out the sound in a word result in unpronounceable groups of consonants – 'tsk', 'zzzt' or 'tchk'. This is inevitable really and all I can suggest is try not to be put off by it, but try to get a feel for how the unpronounceable might sound by listening to the CD. Also our language for describing sound is very limited and subjective, particularly when compared to that for visuals, and so often we rely on visual metaphors.

Another difficulty in talking about bird sounds is that the extent of variation forces one to generalise. Occasionally a bird of any species will produce an unusual variation of its call or song, sometimes even an aberrant version. Sometimes birds, particularly the songbirds, indulge in what might be described as 'playful' variation. This isn't the place to get into the complexities of behavioural interpretation and try to suggest its function, but in such instances individuals seem to be experimenting with the patterns of their vocalisations and voicings almost for its own sake. But this variation is one of the main reasons why an interest in bird sounds so often becomes a lasting fascination for many people.

Where I've given alternative renditions (such as 'wit-a-wit', a thin 'sika' or 'stik-a-lit' for goldfinch calls), sometimes these are borrowed from other listeners' descriptions and may be the same call described or heard differently, but sometimes they are the effect of varied call voicings and possibly even categorically different calls.

Recently ornithologists have been working towards updating the common names of many British species to bring things more in line with names across the international stage. In the text and on the CD I've used the traditional names for species, but given these new species names in brackets.

Songs and calls: repertoires and vocabularies

We've long made an intuitive distinction between songs and calls though in many cases the exact division is not clear. But there's a good behavioural and functional basis to the distinction. Songs are all about performance – a display in sound (and often accompanied by something of a physical show, posturings or movements – song and dance); they are mostly produced by males, generally during the breeding season, indicating an individual's territory, to deter rival males and attract females or keep a mate. They tend to be longer and more complex vocalisations, often in full voice, and are usually performed for long periods for no other apparent reason than their own sake.

Calls on the other hand are mostly produced by either sex, generally all year round, and are more focused on the immediate situation; they tend to be short, simple sounds, though often repeated several times. Calls are most commonly given to contact others or express some degree of unease or outright alarm; warning calls and aggressive calls are also quite frequent.

Song, as just described, is also sometimes referred to as full song – that's to say, the formal version of song produced by a breeding male in full voice. Males 'come into song' with a rise in the testosterone levels in their bodies; in temperate regions, this in turn is triggered by the increasing length of daylight towards spring.

But there are other kinds of song. It used to be that anything other than full song was referred to as subsong; more recently subsong has been restricted to the very soft, inward singing, often continuous and unstructured, occasionally heard from many species. Because such song is so quiet, it's thought to be more frequent than the usual description 'occasionally heard' suggests. Birds singing loudly, but in a looser form than full song, for instance males at the start of their first breeding season, are now said to produce plastic song. Then there's the communal song of a group of birds or even a large flock, again not nearly so structured or full-voiced as full song; and courtship song, excited and usually continuous singing produced by a male in the close presence of a female as a prelude to mating. And females sometimes sing: occasional subsong in many species, but, in the case of robins, for autumn territory.

Some species tend to sing in stereotyped passages – each verse, outburst or strophe (different terms for the same thing) conforms to the same pattern (eg chaffinch, great tit or possibly dunnock). Each pattern is called a song-type and usually an individual bird will have a repertoire of several song-types (cf great tit or yellowhammer songs on the CD). Birds will repeat one song-type for a while, then switch to another song-type, often in response to one of their neighbours' singing. With other species each verse is delivered slightly differently, but conforms to an overall structural pattern (eg blackbird, willow warbler or goldcrest). Then there are species for which each outburst seems completely different, though in a particular style (eg garden warbler, greenfinch or maybe swallow).

Some species sing on the move; or rather, sing a verse from one place, then move on foraging for food before delivering the next verse from a new spot. Others use regular song-posts, usually around the edge of their territories, where they deliver a succession of verses before moving on to another song-post (a high branch, a rooftop or a telephone wire). Singing in verses with intervals between them enables singers to keep a watch for predators and hear rival singers. Birds that sing more continuously, tend to sing from less exposed positions, often within shrubbery or vegetation.

Another difference between songs and calls is that calls are more or less innate, whereas full song, at least among the songbirds, takes a certain amount of practise and listening to other adults. W.H.Thorpe in the 1950s studied the learning process in chaffinches and found that birds reared in isolation produced only a basic form of chaffinch song; even birds which had heard other adults the previous summer, but not since, produced a more accomplished version. This learning process has the effect that song is subject to cultural tradition and there are often idiosyncratic elements in the songs of a species in a particular area, especially with resident species in geographically isolated situations.

Mimicry

Many species include copies of other species calls in their singing. With starlings and some of the warblers mimicry constitutes a large part of their songs. The calls, and sometimes snatches of song, of other species also crop up in the songs of robin, song thrush, blackbird occasionally and some of the finches; and even more so in the case of subsong, which is possibly another indication of its experimental nature.

Song through the seasons

For many of our resident species spring starts early in terms of territoriality and song; mistle thrushes and great tits will sing with increasing frequency on bright or mild days from the winter solstice onwards and starlings have been singing all through. During January blue tits, robins, wrens and gradually dunnock and song thrush will become more vocal, generally later in the north than the south – but all dependent on weather conditions. February and March are the months of the swelling chorus as these species spend more time singing and are joined by others, nuthatch and treecreeper, the woodpeckers drumming, the first blackbird songs and finches exercising with loose meandering songs.

By April the chorus of residents is at a peak and summer visitors are flooding in; May is the peak for residents and visitors alike, with the chorus just after dawn a riot of sound as each male is in full song. June is a turning point as the tit species drop out, busy with their young, and many other species sing less frequently or with longer intervals between songs; it's a good time for listening as there's more space to hear individuals and many warblers and finches should still be singing strongly. But it's a time to know your voices, since the trees are in full leaf to hide the singers.

With July many species wane to silence and moulting; the last week of July and into the start of August is a very quiet time of the birdsong calendar – reserved to swallows and martins, the departing swifts and an occasional finch or bunting. But by the end of August, with the mellowness of the late summer mornings, many species take up a little song again, particularly robins, wrens, dunnock and some of the warblers as they drift south. And of course the unseen wood pigeons that have provided a deep background all summer long. Through October and November robins, wrens and, to a lesser extent, dunnocks are the main singers in gardens; just occasionally on mild days a song thrush might sing out a while and birds of a few other species sing very softly to themselves inside a thick bush or hedge. And before you know it, there's something of a chorus building again in the mid-winter spring.

CONTENTS

CD track numbers appear in brackets

Unless otherwise indicated, recordings are from Northumberland and made by myself. The numbers are for the tracks on the CD. The names that appear in brackets are the internationally recognised common names for the species, as in the British Ornithologists Union list.

ROBIN, WREN, DUNNOCK (1)

These three species can be heard singing or calling at virtually any time of year; and are found in gardens throughout our region. Autumn and early spring is a good time to listen for them, when less other species are in voice.

Robin (European Robin) (2) *Erithacus rubecula*

SONG: A rather high-pitched warble with sudden variations in tempo, in a clear, sharp, ringing voice. Each verse tends to contain some long drawn-out notes and some fast runs with wide variation in pitch. Tuneful in a jazzy way with slurred melodies creating a slightly melancholic or wistful impression. Females take up winter territories in the autumn and sing through that period. Outside the breeding season, song tends to be in a thinner, less strong voice and in less elaborate verses; though sometimes birds are heard singing with an almost continuous warbling in the autumn.

SONG PERIOD: Virtually all year, with a quiet period at the end of July to beginning of August. Song is at its peak from February to June.

CALLS (3): The usual contact and alarm call is a sharp, ringing 'tic', often repeated; sometimes delivered in erratic runs with a chattering quality. Also frequent is a thin, sibilant 'tsee', slightly longer than the similar call of a song thrush.

NOTES: A close relative of the nightingale and, with a less repetitive and athletic song, probably more pleasant and relaxing to listen to, certainly one of my personal favourites. Listen out for occasional mimicry (blackbird rattle in the example on the CD).

RECORDINGS: Song – May; calls – September to November.

Wren (Winter Wren) (4) *Troglodytes troglodytes*

SONG: A surprisingly loud series of repetitive phrases with a clearly-defined structure. Verses are usually 3 to 5 seconds long, rather high-pitched with some sibilant phrases and often a buzzing or rattling phrase. Vibrant and explosive.

SONG PERIOD: Virtually throughout the year, but full song particularly February to July.

CALLS (5): The usual alarm and contact call is a percussive, scratchy 'tchk', voiced singly and run together to produce a rattling sound. Brittle-sounding. Fairly distinctive in Britain: compare it with robin's 'tic's run together, and the fuller-sounding rattle of mistle thrush.

NOTES: A vocal bird throughout the year; can be heard at any time of the day. A restlessly active bird, that rarely delivers more than one or two songs from the same spot. Watch his tail twitch and his wings quiver as he sings. Calls readily in alarm.

RECORDINGS: Song – July (spotted flycatcher, coal tit in background); calls – July and September.

Dunnock (Hedge Accentor) (6) *Prunella modularis*

SONG: A brief, hurried warble, within very limited pitch range. Though superficially rather formless, each delivery is almost identical, so the song is actually quite stereotyped. Verses are often delivered in a quick series of three or four, from one spot then a bird moves on.

SONG PERIOD: The main song period is February to July, but song is frequently heard through the autumn, less so in cold spells.

CALLS (7): The usual contact and alarm call is a clear, surprisingly forceful whistle, 'tsuu', with a light sibilance. A trilled version of this call is also commonly heard, with a tremulous, rather grasshopper-like quality.

NOTES: Readily indulges in subsong, particularly when several birds (two males and a female ?) are near each other in the breeding season. Although quiet, dunnock subsong has a lovely liquid, twittering quality to it.

RECORDINGS: Song – March (with greenfinch close by); calls – February, October and March (great tit, rook in background).

SONG THRUSH, BLACKBIRD, MISTLE THRUSH (8)

These members of the thrush family are all fine singers (quite melodic to our ears) with strong voices. Males generally sing frequently in season, often for quite long periods from favourite, high song-posts.

Song Thrush (9) *Turdus philomelos*

SONG: Strident, clear-toned, far-carrying sound, with a marked repetition of notes and phrases. Varied motifs, common one traditionally rendered 'pretty dick, pretty dick'. Delivery not strictly arranged in verses. Occasional sustained sequences of high-pitched phrases in a thin voice.

SONG PERIOD: February to July; occasional songs heard in autumn.

CALLS (10): The usual alarm call, also often heard from birds going to roost, is a loud rapid-fire 'tsk-tsk-tsk ...', interspersed with softer 'tuk's. The usual contact and flight call is a very unobtrusive, sharp 'tsip' (cf robin 'tsee' call).

NOTES: Listen out for some wonderful arpeggio phrases. Can include some accurate mimicry of other species, particularly nuthatch and buzzard.

RECORDINGS: Song – Aberdeenshire, April (red grouse, black grouse, curlew, coal tit and chaffinch in background); calls – September and May (rook and chaffinch in background).

Blackbird (Common Blackbird) (11) *Turdus merula*

SONG: In well-structured verses, each consisting of one or more melodic flutey phrases that culminate with a thinner-voiced, warbled ending. There is much individual variation apparent even to our ears, with some birds using simple motifs with little variation between verses and other birds showing much more elaborate and varied patterns. The rate of delivery also varies widely: a bird singing at dawn in April (as on the CD) will tend to sing with very short gaps between songs, whereas the same bird singing later in the day, or especially later in the season is likely to space verses further apart.

SONG PERIOD: February to July, beginning later further north; sings less in periods of bad weather.

CALLS (12): Alarm calls range from soft 'pook's, 'tuk's that break into more strident, repeated 'tsk's, similar to song thrush, and a distinctive lilting rattle (often as a bird takes flight). The contact call is a sibilant, slightly trilled 'tssssee'.

NOTES: It is not too difficult to learn to recognise individual birds by distinctive phrases (and their usual songposts), but you have to be a bit careful, since other birds will soon adopt a catchy motif.

RECORDINGS: Song – April; calls – April and March.

Mistle Thrush (13) *Turdus viscivorus*

SONG: Very like blackbird in form and tone, but the opening phrases are more warbled. Verses are shorter and delivered at a swifter pace. Usually sings from a high perch. Motifs are slightly garbled where the blackbird's are clearly enunciated.

SONG PERIOD: Though occasional in December, really gets going in January through to May.

CALLS (14): The alarm and contact call is a quite mechanical rattling sound (think football rattle). Delivery can vary from an even enunciation (which my kids have mistaken for a woodpecker's drumming) to stuttering, slightly squeaky runs from an excited bird, as well as softer calls in flight.

NOTES: Singing in full voice from the highest point of a coppice on a wild day in the early spring, it lives up to its old name – the stormcock.

RECORDINGS: Song – April; calls – May.

BLUE TIT, GREAT TIT, COAL TIT (15)

The members of the tit family are highly vocal birds with wide vocabularies, and many of the incidental contact (brief 'sip's and 'see's) and aggressive calls (hisses and buzzes) are not easy to identify to species. Fortunately each species also has a number of distinctive songs and calls.

Blue Tit (16) *Parus caeruleus*

SONG: High-pitched, repetitive, usually quite sibilant. The commonest form has two or three clear, higher-pitched introductory notes leading into a trill at a slightly lower pitch and of various speeds, such as 'see-see-see-susususu'; there are many slight variations on this theme and either part may be left out. Another form of song features a simple theme repeated over a number of times and there are other motifs delivered in a sort of wheezing squeak.

SONG PERIOD: January to June with a slight resumption in early autumn.

CALLS (17): The most distinctive are an alarm rattle, with a churring quality that rises slightly in pitch and a sharp, petulant 'tch-tch-tch'.

NOTES: With blue tit it is not always easy to separate singing from calling.

RECORDINGS: Song – February and April (oystercatcher and rook in background); calls – February.

Great Tit (18) *Parus major*

SONG: In verses consisting of simple 2- or 3-note ditties repeated over, at a lively pace, though not hurried like coal tit. The notes are tonally subtle, ranging from pure whistles to various slightly metallic or churred sounds, often with a chiming quality. Songs carry well, ringing out beneath a woodland canopy. The motif of the commonest types often rendered 'teacher'.

SONG PERIOD: Mainly January to May; occasional in June and early autumn.

CALLS (19): The most distinctive call is a churring alarm rattle, with a slightly hollow quality and, unlike blue tit, holding an even, low pitch; it is often opened by one or two sharp 'see' notes. Another alarm call is a clear, chaffinch-like 'spink'. But the range of calls heard from great tits is almost infinite, with different ones popular in different areas; the best diagnostic feature is the rich tonal quality of the notes used and neat phrasing.

NOTES: Experienced birders have a saying that, if you hear a call you don't recognise in woodland, it is probably a great tit.

RECORDINGS: Song – Worcestershire, April, Banffshire, May and Northumberland, May; calls – Northumberland, March and February, Kent, February.

Coal Tit (20) *Parus ater*

SONG: Like great tit, in verses consisting of simple 2- or 3-note ditties repeated over, but in a higher-pitched, thinner and possibly sweeter voice; delivered at a more hurried pace than great tit. Commonest type based on a 'wheetu' motif.

SONG PERIOD: Mainly February to June; occasional January and early autumn.

CALLS (21): The most distinctive contact call is a clear-voiced, ringing 'teu', 'teuy' or 'teuy-ti'. Also an alarm and aggressive call – a sibilant rattling or trilled 'ts-ts-ts ...'. But like the previous two species coal tits have quite an armoury of calls not easily separated from those species.

NOTES: Whereas the song might be confused with great tit, the calls are similar to siskin.

RECORDINGS: Song – March; calls – February and March.

NUTHATCH, LONG-TAILED TIT, TREECREEPER, SPOTTED FLYCATCHER (22)

These are more or less woodland species; long-tailed tits may move around through bushes and scrub, but the others tend to be found in the vicinity of stands of mature trees. They are all quite vocal in their own ways.

Nuthatch (Wood Nuthatch) (23) *Sitta europaea*

SONG: Nuthatch song can conveniently be separated into two types: an evenly-trilled note, and a series of evenly enunciated 'twee' notes, verses of each type being repeated at intervals.

SONG PERIOD: Late winter through to late spring.

CALLS (24): The commonest calls are a distinctive, loud 'twit' or 'twoit', sometimes delivered in quick series of two's or three's, and various sharp, sibilant 'tsee's, not easily differentiated from similar calls from a range of other species, but quite distinctive with practise. Other calls include a descending 'tyu' (possibly a song variant), similar to a willow tit's song, but with a typically nuthatch strident flutey tone; a rapid 'tutututu ...' in alarm.

NOTES: Generally quite a vocal bird, with a lovely rich and distinctive voice – a good species to learn to recognise if they are in your area.

RECORDINGS: Song – April (rook, mistle thrush and carrion crow in background); calls – July.

Long-tailed Tit (25) *Aegithalus caudatus*

SONG: A soft, rather subdued twittering warble is sometimes heard. But there's no record of a formal song.

CALLS: The main calls are a sharp 'tchup', a trilling 'trrrr' and a high-pitched sibilant 'tsee', often given in series, especially in a run of 3 or 4, slightly descending in pitch.

NOTES: Very vocal birds, as they are sociable, whether foraging in a winter flock, moving as a pair in spring or in a family party, long-tailed tits are rarely quiet; they tend to keep in touch calling every few seconds. This activity seems to draw birds of other species to the flock, so it is always worth observing to see what else is moving with them, particularly in autumn and winter.

RECORDINGS: Northumberland, August and Worcestershire, April.

Treecreeper (Eurasian Treecreeper) (26) *Certhia familiaris*

SONG: In verses with a chaffinch-like pattern of accelerating trills ending with a brief flourish, voiced with a wren-like sibilance closer to the pitch of a goldcrest.

SONG PERIOD: Can be heard from late winter to early summer.

CALLS (27): The most noticeable call is a series of high-pitched, shiveringly-sibilant trills. Usually quite drawn-out and often in a regularly-spaced series. Birds tend to call every few seconds with a very soft little 'swit', not particularly diagnostic, but often useful to alert you to an unseen bird close-by.

NOTES: In suitably wooded areas (not necessarily woodland, but with mature trees) this is often a more common species than is at first apparent. Although it is unobtrusive and constantly on the move foraging its way up the trunk and branches of trees, it is quite confiding and has a subtle charm of its own. Its song and calls are the best indicator of its whereabouts, since birds tend to call at regular intervals.

RECORDINGS: Song – March (wood pigeon and mistle thrush in background); calls – Worcestershire, March.

Spotted Flycatcher (28) *Muscicapa striata*

SONG: Song is little more than quicker excited repetition of the brief, sibilant call notes, with slight pitching variations and some notes trilled. Occasionally males break into a rapid soft warbling when courting a nearby female.

SONG PERIOD: May to June.

CALLS (29): The main call is a shrill, often slightly tremulous 'tsee'. Birds call with a 'tsee-tch-tch' when alarmed.

NOTES: Despite the limited vocabulary and voicing, this is generally quite a vocal species – certainly from their spring arrival through the main part of the summer.

RECORDINGS: Song – May; calls – June.

SWIFT, SWALLOW, HOUSE MARTIN, PIED WAGTAIL (30)

All rather vocal species, without particularly formal songs.

Swift (Common Swift) (31) *Apus apus*

VOICE: A high-pitched, trilled 'scream', uttered either singly or in quick series. Sometimes single birds are heard to call, but more often a group of birds are heard calling in a wild, high-speed chase – particularly in late evening in summer. Birds call throughout their time on their breeding grounds – May to early August.

NOTES: Although similar in form and behaviour to house martin and swallow, swifts belong to a non-passerine family, more closely related to nightjars and even kingfishers than these two hirundines. So it is probably not surprising that their calls show no elaboration comparable to the songbirds.

RECORDINGS: July.

Swallow (Barn Swallow) (32) *Hirundo rustica*

SONG: Continuous passages of lively twittering, including every now and then a very distinctive, lip-smacking, drawn-out buzz. Although the twittering at first appears formless and meandering, after listening a while, one begins to recognise repeated patterns. Birds sing in flight and perched.

SONG PERIOD: Throughout the summer and possibly in winter too.

CALLS (33): The usual contact call is a brief 'whit' or 'whit-whit', sometimes more of a 'chit'. The alarm call is a wagtail-like 'chissik'. Another alarm call is given in a distinctive motif sounding something like 'choy-cheewi', though voicings vary.

NOTES: One of the characteristic sounds of summer – from farmyards to suburban lawns.

RECORDINGS: Song – July (jackdaw in background); calls – July and August (collared dove in background).

House Martin (34) *Delichon urbica*

SONG: A fairly continuous stream of chirruping and twittering; sounds like a stream of call notes, with chattering variation. Birds sing for longer periods perched by or in the nest; and in occasional short snatches in flight. Quite pleasant and musical.

SONG PERIOD: Much of the spring and summer.

CALLS (35): The usual call, frequently given in flight, is a brief dry rattling trill. Also a slurred 'tseurr', probably an alarm call.

NOTES: Listen out for the massed voices of a large flock calling in excitement.

RECORDINGS: Song – by David Burton, North Devon, June; calls – August.

Pied Wagtail (36) *Motacilla alba*

SONG: Birds are not heard singing often, but do occasionally break into passages of quite subdued twittering. This tends to sound as if it is coming from a more distant source than the actual bird.

SONG PERIOD: Probably mostly spring to summer.

CALLS: Main contact and alarm call an abrupt 'chissik', often given in flight. Also 'cheeup' in alarm near nest or young. Birds often spend time voicing variations on their call at regular intervals every few seconds; this may be a kind of singing.

NOTES: Often heard calling from rooftops in towns, even through winter. Listen out for roosting flocks in winter around service stations, hotels, supermarkets and bus stations.

RECORDINGS: Song – July (wood pigeon and rook in background); calls – Sutherland, April.

CHAFFINCH AND YELLOWHAMMER (38)

Both have formal or stereotyped songs – each delivery of a particular song-type is more or less identical, though a bird may have a repertoire of several different types.

Chaffinch (39) *Fringilla coelebs*

SONG: A short series of three or four quickly-repeated notes or trills, accelerating in pace and ending in a slight flourish; imaginatively compared by Warde Fowler to the changing rhythms in the steps of a bowler in cricket as he takes his run up. Verses are around 2 to 3 seconds in length and delivered in a rich voice from a perch; the sound carries well. Males usually have a repertoire of several different song types and reiterate one for several minutes before switching to another type. This gives a repetitive impression to the song.

SONG PERIOD: Mainly February to June; occasional in July and September.

CALLS (40): The main contact and flight call is a softish 'chiff' or 'tupe'; the usual alarm call a strident 'spink' or 'chink'. Males in the breeding season often repeat a 'huit' or 'weet' call at short intervals for long periods.

NOTES: Chaffinches are widespread wherever there are a few shrubs or trees; they sing persistently from a medium height song-post and their song is quite distinct. A good species for beginners to learn.

RECORDINGS: Song – Aberdeenshire, May; calls – Aberdeenshire, May and February.

Yellowhammer (41) *Emberiza citrinella*

Song: A brief rather grasshopper-like slow trill, rises slightly in pitch and culminates in one or two languid notes. The repeated notes of the trill tend to have a rather metallic ringing or scraping quality (typical for buntings). The traditional mnemonic 'a little bit of bread and no chee-eese' gives a good impression of the rhythm, but doesn't fit all song renditions or types exactly; birds often drop the last two 'cheese' notes.

Song period: From February to August.

Calls (42): The most distinctive contact and alarm call, also used in flight, is a brief liquid trill sounding something like 'trrilip'. A terse, buzzing 'zzt', similar to some of the other buntings is frequent and a slightly sharper 'zit' is slightly more distinctive (unless you're in a cirl bunting area).

Notes: Yellowhammer songs have a simple beauty that conjures up overgrown quiet lanes in summer with the sun spreading a lazy heat on all.

Recordings: Song – Morayshire, May and Northumberland, July; calls – December and May.

Greenfinch, Goldfinch, Siskin, Linnet (43)

These finches belong to the carduelis genus, different from chaffinch, and their breeding behaviour is not so strictly territorial as chaffinch. They are all lovely singers, with varied, trilled and twittering songs, and were popular as caged song-birds in the past.

Greenfinch (European Greenfinch) (44) *Carduelis chloris*

Song: The full song of males is a fairly continuous, meandering series of trills, with endless variations on the call notes, occasional tinkling sounds, repeated sweet 'teu-teu-teu's interspersed with sustained, buzzing 'dzweee's, all delivered in a rich, canary-like voice. Birds also spend long periods in spring and summer voicing just the buzzy 'dzwee' sound at regular intervals.

Song period: Mainly February to July.

Calls (45): Many and various trilled repetitions of a slightly hard, percussive 'chip' note; sometimes voiced singly. Various renditions of a sweet 'tooey' note are also common.

Notes: A lovely background singer – quite canary-like in voice.

Recordings: Song – Northumberland, March and Oxfordshire, July; calls – February and July (collared dove and house sparrow in background).

Goldfinch (European Goldfinch) (46) *Carduelis carduelis*

SONG: A steady, fast succession of trills, repeated liquid notes and brief wheezes, usually opening with call phrases, in a delivery suggesting real passion. The rather long verses may at first appear to meander, but, with repeated listening to an individual bird, reveal a formal structure with sequences of phrases being repeated often exactly. A looser form of song, building variations around call phrases, is also heard from groups of birds and a communal twittering from flocks.

SONG PERIOD: Full song from April to August. Loose song almost any time of year, but particularly early spring and early autumn.

CALLS (47): The usual contact and flight call is an effortless, liquid-toned 'wit-a-wit', a thin 'sika' or 'stik-a-lit'. Other calls include a sweet rising 'chooy' and 'cheweeu' in a similar voice, and a rattling buzz, given in aggression – often heard when a goldfinch is at the feeder.

NOTES: The collective term for a group of goldfinches is a 'charm', probably with the same root as 'carmen', the latin for song or poem.

RECORDINGS: Song – May; calls – April, Aug and April (collared dove and rook in backgrounds).

Siskin (Eurasian Siskin) (48) *Carduelis spinus*

SONG: An extended medley of twittering or chattering, full of mimicry of other species (especially song thrush alarm calls), usually including a distinctive drawn-out wheezing note and maybe an arpeggiated trill. The whole delivery is at a steady, swift pace. On the breeding grounds males often sing a less frenetic version in a fluttering song-flight. Outside spring and summer birds in small parties may sing with a looser twittering; and sometimes a mass communal babble is heard from winter flocks.

SONG PERIOD: Mainly February to June. Loose twittering all year round.

CALLS (49): The main calls are a clear, descending 'teu' or 'tsu', quite plaintive sounding and often given in flight, a rising, wheezy 'teuy' or 'tzuy' and 'teuy-li' and a sharp, chattering 'tchk'.

NOTES: The song, though vibrant, is not particularly loud and is easily overlooked, especially if there are a few other species singing or calling in the vicinity. It is probably at its sweetest in songflight, though this is less often heard in gardens – other than those bordering pinewoods.

RECORDINGS: Song – March; calls – Aberdeenshire, May (willow warbler in background).

Linnet (Common Linnet) (50) *Carduelis cannabina*

SONG: A medley of rhythmic percussive notes, slightly buzzing and tinkling trills and sweet melodic phrases delivered at a lively even pace. Reminiscent of both greenfinch (but livelier) and goldfinch (but steadier), and more varied and musical than either. Verses, often lasting 3 to 5 seconds, may be delivered for periods at even intervals and occasional build to more sustained continuous passages.

SONG PERIOD: Full song April to July, looser song early spring and autumn.

CALLS (51): The usual flight and alarm call is a sharp 'chic', like pebbles knocked together, generally given in short rhythmic motifs, often 'chic-a-chic'.

NOTES: Another personal favourite with its lovely oblique melodies.

RECORDINGS: Song – June; calls – Fife, July.

BULLFINCH, HAWFINCH (52)

These two species share characteristics in their vocal behaviour differing from the other finches. Although they are generally quite vocal, calling readily and often singing in a kind of varied subsong typical of the cardueline finches, males of neither species have anything like a loud, formal song. Hence though their calls are very useful (almost essential with hawfinches) for locating or identifying unseen birds, song is really only of aesthetic or academic interest.

Bullfinch (Common Bullfinch) (53) *Pyrrhula pyrrhula*

SONG: Males occasionally give quite a loud, drawn-out whistle on an even pitch, which may be a kind of song. More often song is a soft, usually very soft, piping with variations on a theme; it may include churring buzzes and twittering notes. Males indulge in such song quite frequently, females occasionally with possibly a simpler form.

SONG PERIOD: The subsong can probably be heard at any time of year, but is most common and strongest in spring and summer.

CALLS (54): The usual contact and alarm call is a rich, piped 'tyoo' or 'dyu', a good indicator of the bird's presence nearby. A slightly more clipped version is given in flight and a range of similar calls are heard on occasion, with a hint of the same tonal quality. A softer, brief 'yhu' contact call is often heard when birds are feeding.

NOTES: Although not audible at any distance, bullfinch song has a charm of its own and is really quite haunting.

RECORDINGS: Song – Worcestershire, March; calls – April and February.

Hawfinch (55) *Coccothraustes coccothraustes*

SONG: Singing birds string together a medley of sounds incorporating renditions of the 'tzic' call and drawn-out, slightly tremulous, shrill 'tseu'-type notes, alternating with softer clicks and buzzes; sometimes longer bouts of the subsong are delivered in courtship with a weird variety of soft guttural sounds produced.

SONG PERIOD: Mainly spring.

CALLS: The contact and alarm call is an explosive 'tzic'.

NOTES: The call needs careful separation from robin 'tic's.

RECORDINGS: Worcestershire, March.

GARDEN WARBLER, BLACKCAP, WILLOW WARBLER, CHIFFCHAFF, GOLDCREST (56)

Although they may sing from a static perch on occasions or for a short period, these warblers tend to move on and feed between verses.

Garden Warbler (57) *Sylvia borin*

SONG: A hurried, bubbling warble generally weaving around an even pitch. Steady, very brisk tempo. Occasional extended 'falsetto' sections. The voice is slightly trilled compared to blackcap and it is difficult to detect any regular structure to the song verses.

SONG PERIOD: May to July.

CALLS (58): The usual alarm call is a scratchy 'tchek' usually repeated at quite a fast, regular rate; also various low churred notes.

NOTES: Frequently sings from within bushes or at shrub height but not always.

RECORDINGS: Song – June (wood pigeon, tree pipit, wren and willow warbler in background); calls – July (chaffinch in background).

Blackcap (59) *Sylvia atricapilla*

SONG: A sprightly warble, delivered in verses (sometimes extended), with variations in pace and a wide range of pitching and phrasing; verses usually begin hesitantly with a medley of thin-voiced scratchy and buzzy notes and build in rhythm towards the end with clearer-toned, slightly flutey notes in a recognisable motif. Although often rather complex, verses give the impression of more overall structure in contrast with garden warbler's meandering from start to arbitrary stop.

SONG PERIOD: April to July. Occasionally in September

CALLS (60): The usual alarm call is a sharp, tongue-clicking 'tchk'.

NOTES: Song complexity varies a lot between individuals and time of year. Beware of occasional outbursts of robins in blackcap style.

RECORDINGS: Song – July; calls – July.

Willow Warbler (61) *Phylloscopus trochilus*

SONG: In shortish tumbling verses of sweet, slurred, flutey notes delivered at a steady, unhurried pace. Verses usually consist in a series of phrases, descending in pitch to an ending flourish, quite chaffinch-like in structure. A frequent and persistent singer.

SONG PERIOD: April to July. Occasional in September.

CALLS (62): The usual contact and alarm call is a disyllabic, clear-toned 'hooeet'. Also a range of wheezing notes as in the example on the CD.

NOTES: Tends to sing at shrub- to mid-height.

RECORDINGS: Song – Aberdeenshire, May; calls – Sutherland, June.

Chiffchaff (Common Chiffchaff) (63) *Phylloscopus collybita*

SONG: A slightly halting series of 'chiff-chaff'-like notes, deliberately enunciated, each verse lasting around four or five seconds. But not always in 2-note motifs. Birds often deliver a ticking call between verses (as on the CD), especially in early spring. At a slower pace and tonally different from great tit.

SONG PERIOD: Late March to July. Occasional in September.

CALLS (64): The usual contact and alarm call is a single rising note 'huit' with just a hint of a shrill wheeziness.

NOTES: Tends to sing from higher up in trees than willow warbler. Also compare with great tit song.

RECORDINGS: Song – Worcestershire, March; call – September.

Goldcrest (65) *Regulus regulus*

SONG: A 3- or 4-note motif is repeated at a fast pace with building momentum before ending with a final flourish – all in a very high-pitched, quite squeaky voice. The ending may be a brief trill or a tit-like phrase and is varied from verse to verse, but is sometimes omitted. Each verse generally lasts around 3–4 seconds and intervals between them can be quite short.

SONG PERIOD: Mainly February to July, with a resumption in the autumn.

CALLS (66): A wide range of thin, high-pitched notes, some cleanly-voiced, others slightly trilled, and varying in length; calls are often in a brief, rhythmic run.

NOTES: Generally a very vocal bird for much of the year, but it is easily overlooked because of its very high-pitched voice.

RECORDINGS: Song – July and April; calls – April.

House Sparrow, Starling (67)

These two species are often found around houses and are both vocal and vociferous.

House Sparrow (68) *Passer domesticus*

SONG: House sparrows have no song with any apparent formal structure. But males spend long periods delivering an endless series of chirps and chirrups each with slight variation and at a deliberate, steady pace. The delivery speeds up and becomes more excited in courtship and in disputes.

SONG PERIOD: All year round.

CALLS (69): Quite a wide vocabulary of calls include 'chow', chattering 'chek's and rattles in alarm, a slightly trilled 'tyu' and a soft 'tsee'.

NOTES: Generally a very vocal species; easily overlooked possibly because its voice is not so musical to our ears. And yet the social life of house sparrows can be very entertaining.

RECORDINGS: Song – April; calls – March and June.

Starling (Common Starling) (70) *Sturnus vulgaris*

SONG: Though starling song may appear unstructured and birds spend much time singing casually, individuals do develop a formal rendition. Generally beginning with a medley of mimicry, with possibly a few 'signature' whistles as a prelude, the pace builds into passages of rapid bill-clicking, repeated shrill whistles and throaty wheezes.

SONG PERIOD: August/September right through to May.

CALLS (71): Starlings produce many strange calls at times, when they just seem to be playing with sound. The main alarm calls are a sharp buzzing 'tzik' or 'tizza' and a churring 'tcharrr', often repeated, and generally given at an intruder round the nest.

NOTES: It always strikes me as something of a vocal harlequin; it is a pity that the best bits of their song are delivered quite quietly. The songs on the CD include mimicry of herring gull, song thrush, blackbird, rook, jackdaw, dunnock and greenfinch, then kestrel, curlew, lapwing, golden plover and car alarms.

RECORDINGS: Song – February (house sparrow, collared dove in background); calls – May.

Magpie, Jay, Jackdaw, Carrion Crow (72)

All these species are members of the crow family and have a much more extensive and subtle repertoire of vocalisations than is at first apparent. Their territorial and contact calls, generally loud and rough sounds, are quite well-known; but they all indulge more or less in bouts of subsong producing a wide variety of guttural clicks, squeals, moans and chattering often with almost human enunciations.

Magpie (Black-billed Magpie) (73) *Pica pica*

The characteristic call is a powerful chuckling rattle; sometimes brief rhythmic motifs are uttered in the same voice, or incorporating a squeal, and an explosive disyllabic variation. Birds sing with a quiet inward chuckling and squeaking.

RECORDINGS: Cumbria, by Roger Boughton and Worcestershire, April.

Jay (Eurasian Jay) (74) *Garrulus glandarius*

The diagnostic call is a hoarse squawk, but there are 2 versions: an out-and-out harsh shriek, and commonly a more controlled magpie-like call, often given as a double. There are various voicings to this latter and it can merge into the softer churrings, guttural clucks and squeals of subsong. Jays are also excellent mimics, one of their favourite copies being buzzard calls.

RECORDINGS: Worcestershire, April.

Jackdaw (Eurasian Jay) (75) *Corvus monedula*

Wide variations on a basic explosive, slightly hoarse 'jaah' or 'tchew'; sometimes very gruff, and sometimes almost disyllabic ('jee-ah'). Very vocal; particularly around nest site and small groups in flight (joy-flighting).

RECORDINGS: June and January.

Carrion Crow (76) *Corvus corone*

The usual territorial and general contact call is a series of harsh, rattly 'kaa's; in contrast rooks have a softer, more churring tone of voice. But carrion crows sometimes utter odd, slightly honky versions of the call in display and such calls may form part of their subsong. The alarm call, given when chasing any potential predator, is a throaty rattle.

RECORDINGS: March (grey partridge).

SPARROWHAWK, KESTREL (77)

Many of the hawk and falcon species have two main ways of calling: a petulant-sounding repeated 'kecking' or 'yikkering' and a shrill squealing or mewing, again often repeated.

Sparrowhawk (Eurasian Sparrowhawk) (78) *Accipiter nisus*

Generally a silent species other than around the nest site. Birds will call quite readily in alarm at an intruder into the nesting area; the usual calls are a rapid, petulant yikkering and a rather high-pitched squealing. Males bringing in food call to the female with a rather softer version of the yikkering call and the female generally answers with a slight mew. The first time I heard the yikkering call, it reminded me of a light-weight green woodpecker's yaffle; shortly afterwards a sparrowhawk arrived in tree close-by and quickly spotted me with its sharp yellow eye, but that was enough for me to realise the source of the call I'd heard.

RECORDINGS: June and July.

Kestrel (Common Kestrel) (79) *Falco tinnunculus*

Like sparrowhawks and many other raptors, this species is most vocal around the nest-site; but you do hear kestrels giving the 'kecking' call at other times occasionally, often for no apparent reason. The usual call is a shrill, penetrating 'kek-kek-kek' in a burst of 1 or 2 seconds. Around the nest shivering squeals are heard and sharp clicks in courtship.

RECORDINGS: Banffshire, May.

WOOD PIGEON, COLLARED DOVE, TURTLE DOVE, CUCKOO (80)

The pigeons and doves sing readily with their simple cooing patterns, but do not usually use calls – collared dove is an exception. Cuckoo is included for its similar-sounding voice and though various sounds are heard in spring other than the call, cuckoos are pretty quiet at other times. Turtle dove and cuckoo are summer visitors.

Wood Pigeon (Common Wood Pigeon) (81) *Columba palumbus*

SONG: A deep leisurely cooing in a rather husky voice (certainly when heard close-to) usually to the rhythm of 'take two coo's, taffy'. The song can be heard for much of the year, though not often in winter. A single, repeated long crooning note is also heard in summer. Wood pigeons also have a wing-clapping display flight – a characteristic sound that many people will be familiar with, as well as the clatter of wings from flushed birds.

RECORDINGS: Worcestershire, April (wren in background).

Collared Dove (Eurasian Collared Dove) (82) *Streptopelia decaocto*

SONG: A far-carrying, resonant cooing to the rhythm of 'that's nice, Pip', though there are other themes heard. Occasionally mistaken for cuckoo, it also has a similar tone to tawny owl hoots. There's a wheezing flight call, generally given by birds coming in to land.

Turtle Dove (European Turtle Dove) (83) *Streptopelia turtur*

SONG: A purring motif like 'oo-cu-hoo' is repeated over in continuous passages of around 10-20 seconds. There's fair variation in the motif between different birds. Several birds can sound like a chorus of frogs in the distance.

RECORDINGS: Kent, June (sedge warbler and reed warbler in background).

Cuckoo (Common Cuckoo) (84) *Cuculus canorus*

SONG: The male's song sounds just like the bird's name repeated over, sometimes for longish periods. Occasionally 3-note versions are heard. It is said that they change their tune in June: it is more like their voice begins to go. Birds also make soft cackling and spitting sounds when excited. Females have a slightly hysterical-sounding bubbling call in the breeding season.

RECORDINGS: Scandinavia, by Roger Boughton.

TAWNY OWL, LITTLE OWL, BARN OWL (85)

Owl voices vary from pure hoots, to wailing mews, screeches and hisses. Tawny and little owls are vocal species and heard throughout the year, barn owl less so.

Tawny Owl (86) *Strix aluco*

SONG: A full round hooting sound, often clear-toned but sometimes husky, that carries well and is heard all year round. In its formal version, delivered in 2 parts – 'hooo' followed several seconds later by a broken hooting phrase. Also a wavering, drawn-out softer hoot; often heard at nightfall. Females sing occasionally.

CALL: The usual contact and alarm call is a sharp 'kewick', sometimes repeated as 'wick-wick-wick'. Odd versions of this call are heard from juveniles in summer. Also some mewing wails are heard from birds in encounters.

RECORDINGS: June and March (roe deer, rook, jackdaw in background).

Little Owl (87) *Athene noctua*

SONG: A short hoot which holds a pitch, then rises at the end. Higher-pitched and thinner sounding than tawny.

CALLS: Alarm calls include explosive 'keuk's, sometimes confusable with tawny 'kwick's, and yelps. Other calls include various mewing sounds and scratchy hisses.

RECORDINGS: Northumberland, May; Dorset, by Kyle Turner; Northumberland, June.

Barn Owl (88) *Tyto alba*

CALLS vary from the 'snoring' hisses of young birds to the scratchy or screeching hisses of territorial adults. But barn owls are generally quite silent birds away from the nest site and not often heard calling.

RECORDINGS: Lincolnshire, September by Phil Rudkin (red deer in background).

GREAT SPOTTED WOODPECKER, LESSER SPOTTED WOODPECKER, GREEN WOODPECKER (89)

The woodpeckers are named from their well-known habit of hammering on wood with their bills. In the course of hollowing out a nesting hole or trying to reach a wood-boring grub for food, this is likely to be a steady tapping and probably not particularly loud since the wood will need to be reasonably soft. The rapid burst of hard taps known as 'drumming' is a territorial and courtship signal, like song in other species, and has no wood-cutting function; so hard resonant wood should provide the best drumming surfaces.

Great Spotted Woodpecker (90) *Dendrocopos major*

SONG: A short (usually less than 1 second), evenly-timed burst of drumming that fades to the end. Performed by both male and female. Sometimes metal objects like poles or drain pipes are used.

SONG PERIOD: Generally February to May.

CALLS (91): Calls readily in alarm at intruders or when disturbed with loud, sharp 'pip's, sometimes sounding thicker, like 'tchik'; occasionally given in quick, tittering runs.

RECORDINGS: Drumming – Inverness-shire, May (wood warbler, great tit in background); calls – Worcestershire, March.

Lesser Spotted Woodpecker (92) *Dendrocopos minor*

SONG: A slightly longer (usually over 1 second) burst of drumming than great spotted, that holds its level to an abrupt end. Generally quieter than great spotted. But it is not easy to tell the two species apart with certainty on drumming alone.

SONG PERIOD: Generally February to May.

CALLS: Has a sharp 'pip'-type call similar to great spotted but generally quieter and thinner-sounding; and less often heard. More distinctive and more frequently-heard is a shrill, strident 'ki-ki-ki- ...' call, often compared to kestrel and the much rarer wryneck.

RECORDINGS: Worcestershire, April.

Green Woodpecker (93) *Picus viridis*

SONG: A loud, quick, even run of 'klee' notes, subsiding towards the end and sounding like a fit of giggling – the 'yaffle' (also the bird's old colloquial name). Repeated every few minutes.

SONG PERIOD: Most frequent from late winter through spring.

CALLS: Flight and alarm calls sound similar to the yaffle, but not so formally delivered – often given as doubles, 'klee-klee'. Repeated more urgently and higher-pitched in alarm.

RECORDINGS: April (rook, blackbird, chaffinch in background).

PHEASANT

Pheasant (Common Pheasant) (94) *Phasianus colchicus*

SONG: The male's formal territorial signal is a brief, loud, harsh crowing motif followed by a powerful wing flutter, heard most frequently through the spring; quite distinctive, far-carrying and easily recognised. Through the rest of the year similar crowing notes at regular intervals and rapid outbursts of crowing are heard often at dusk and to a lesser extent at dawn. Through the spring males also often utter a pulsing moan while foraging and particularly when a female is in the vicinity.

CALLS: Males also give the repeated crowing call when flushed; females sometimes give a sharp squeak. Both sexes give soft, squeaky, wheezing calls.

RECORDINGS: April, February (with mallard), April and October.

GREY HERON, COOT, MOORHEN, KINGFISHER (95)

As with many waterside birds, these are all quite vocal species, though herons spend long periods silent when hunting or snoozing.

Grey Heron (96) *Ardea cinerea*

Grey herons are very vocal around their nesting colonies, voicing a range of deep shrieks, caws and bill-clattering sounds. When disturbed or in encounters with other herons, birds frequently call with a barking shriek ('frank') voiced either singly or in a subsiding series of 4 or 5.

RECORDINGS: France, June (greenfinch and blackcap in background); Cumbria, by Roger Boughton.

Coot (Common Coot) (97) *Fulica atra*

Coots spend more time in open water than moorhens so are generally more obvious to the eye. Nevertheless they are a very vocal species especially during the early part of the breeding season. The main call is a series of loud explosive 'kowp's, variable in voicing, sometimes shrill 'keuk's; frequently this follows or leads to territorial disputes with splashing runs across the surface of the water. They also produce a range of unusual sharp, very abrupt sounds, such as 'phut', 'pit' and 'seet'.

RECORDINGS: Dumfrieshire, April (with great crested grebe at start); Northumberland, April (willow warbler, long-tailed tit and mistle thrush in background).

Moorhen (Common Moorhen) (98) *Gallinula chloropus*

Moorhens have two very loud explosive calls, both as far as I know always voiced as single utterances: a brief bubbling 'prrrt' and a sharp, abrupt 'chid' or 'chidda'. Both are fairly distinctive and though the latter is roughly similar to some coot sounds, coots tend to repeat the calls in a series. More difficult to distinguish is moorhen's repeated hollow 'huc' calls, variable in loudness and sometimes given in a spluttering outburst: the 'huc's are often heard at dusk and even into the darkness. Moorhens spend much time creeping about in rank vegetation, so the calls are a very useful indicator of a bird's presence.

RECORDINGS: January.

Kingfisher (Common Kingfisher) (99) *Alcedo atthis*

The usual call is a beautiful, thin, but quite powerful whistle, often descending slightly in pitch. It is reminiscent of a dunnock's call, so think twice if you hear a dunnock by a river or pond. Birds often call in flight, so familiarity with the call is really useful for drawing your attention to a bird which, despite its gorgeous colouring, is easily missed. Kingfishers occasionally sing with playful repeated variations around the call note.

RECORDINGS: France, June (cuckoo, reed warbler, chiffchaff and nightingale in background).

INDEX OF COMMON NAMES

INDEX OF LATIN NAMES